W9-AQZ-698

MONSTERS

BY DON NARDO
AND BRADLEY STEFFENS

KIDHAVEN PRESS
An imprint of Thomson Gale, a part of The Thomson Corporation

THOMSON
GALE ™

Detroit • New York • San Francisco • San Diego • New Haven, Conn.
Waterville, Maine • London • Munich

For Wynona

For more information, contact
KidHaven Press
27500 Drake Rd.
Farmington Hills, MI 48331–3535
Or you can visit our Internet site at http://www.gale.com

LIBRARY OF CONGRESS CATALOGING–IN–PUBLICATION DATA

Nardo, Don, 1947–
Cyclops / by Don Nardo and Bradley Steffens
p. cm. — (Monsters)
Includes bibliographical references and index.
ISBN 0–7377–2615–6 (hardcover : alk. paper)
1. Cyclopes (Greek mythology)—Juvenile literature. I. Title. II. Monsters series (KidHaven Press)
BL820.C83N37 2004
398.2'0938'01—dc22 2004010970

Printed in the United States of America

Contents

Chapter 1

The Terror of Greece

The people who lived in Greece more than twenty–five thousand years ago believed the universe was inhabited by many gods, demigods, and monsters. Many Greek monsters were savage and cruel. For example, the centaurs–creatures with the torso of a man and the body of a horse–ate raw flesh, drank a lot, and attacked women. Another monster, the Minotaur, had the body of a man and the head of a bull. It was kept imprisoned in an elaborate maze known as the Labyrinth and was fed seven young women and seven young men every nine years. Perhaps the most loathsome of the Greek monsters were the Cyclopes (si–KLOH–peez), a race of giants who, like the Minotaur, had a taste for human flesh.

The term *Cyclops* comes from the Greek word *kuklos,* meaning "circle." It refers to the Cyclops's most unusual feature–a single, round eye that gaped from the center of its forehead. The eye of the Cyclops set it apart from all other monsters.

A marble bust from ancient Greece shows the one–eyed monster known as the Cyclops.

Legends Based on Fact?

The early Greek storytellers most likely used their imaginations to make up stories about creatures like the Cyclopes. However, some modern scholars believe these fantastic stories may have come from discoveries made in Greece and surrounding islands.

The Minotaur, a mythical creature that was part man and part bull, feeds on flesh in this modern painting.

Elephant skulls like this one were thought to be the remains of Cyclopes.

"The ancient Greeks were farmers and would certainly come across fossil bones . . . and try to explain them," says Thomas Strasser, an **archaeologist** at California State University in Sacramento. "With no concept of evolution, it makes sense that they would reconstruct them in their minds as giants, monsters, sphinxes, and so on."[1]

One type of fossil in particular may have led to the legend of the Cyclopes. Sometimes Greek farmers came across huge skulls that had a large circular pit in the middle of the face. The Greeks may have thought this large hole was an eye socket, giving rise to the idea of one–eyed giants. Actually these skulls belonged to an extinct form of elephant that had once roamed Greece. The circular opening was the place where the creature's trunk was attached.

The Greeks also were awed by the remains of some ancient stone walls. Some of the stones in these walls weighed many tons. The stones were so large, the Greeks reasoned, that only giants could have lifted them. For this reason, these walls came to be called "Cyclopean" after the Cyclopes. Archaeologists now know that the walls were built by ordinary humans who lived in an earlier Greek age. The era of these wall builders is known as the **Bronze Age**, because people in those days used tools and weapons made of bronze. Perhaps distorted memories of Greece's Bronze Age gave rise to the legend of the Cyclopes.

The ancient Greeks believed that the Cyclopes built these massive stone walls.

The First Cyclopes

Whatever the source of the legends, the Greek poet Hesiod, who lived around 700 B.C., wrote that the first generation of Cyclopes were the children of Gaia ("Mother Earth") and Uranus ("the Sky"). In his epic poem ***Theogony***, which means "the family lineage of the gods," Hesiod wrote that Gaia and Uranus had eighteen children–twelve Titans, three giants, and three Cyclopes. The Cyclopes were named Brontes ("Thunder"), Steropes ("Lightning"), and Arges ("Shining One"). The first Cyclopes were giants with great physical power.

Brontes, Steropes, and Arges were skilled metalsmiths who made weapons. They also learned how to capture sources of energy such as thunder and lightning. These skills made the first Cyclopes very powerful. This worried their father. He feared that his children might try to overthrow him. To make sure this never happened, Uranus locked the Cyclopes in Tartarus, the lowest and darkest part of the Underworld.

Cronos, the youngest and boldest of the Titans, also recognized the power of the Cyclopes. Wanting to overthrow his father, Cronos released Brontes, Steropes, and Arges from Tartarus. Together the Titans and the Cyclopes overthrew Uranus. Cronos became the king of the gods. Like his father, however, Cronos began to fear the Cyclopes. He decided to imprison them in Tartarus, just as Uranus had.

The War in Heaven

Brontes, Steropes, and Arges were not destined to spend eternity in the darkness of Tartarus, however. Zeus, one of the sons of Cronos, freed them from their underground prison. Like Cronos, Zeus wanted to overthrow his own father. Zeus gathered together his brothers and sisters, as well as the Cyclopes and other creatures he freed from Tartarus. With these allies at his side, Zeus challenged Cronos and the Titans for control of the universe.

As the battle raged, the Cyclopes supplied Zeus with powerful weapons–thunder and lightning. According to Hesiod, these weapons turned the tide of the battle: "From Zeus's mighty hand, the bolts kept flying, bringing thunder–claps and lightning–flashes. . . . The flashing brightness of the thunderbolt and lightning blinded all, however strong."[2]

The End of the First Cyclopes

After the defeat of the Titans, Zeus established a new order of gods. He took them to live atop Mount Olympus, the tallest mountain in Greece. These gods became known as the Olympians. The Cyclopes were happy to serve as followers and helpers of Zeus. However, they got caught up in a **feud** between Zeus and Apollo, god of prophecy and light.

Apollo had a son with a mortal woman named Coronis. The boy, Asclepius, grew up to be skilled in the art of healing. One day Asclepius used his

The god Zeus hurls lightning bolts as he battles Cronos and the Titans for control of the universe.

powers to bring a dead person back to life. This act, although amazing, broke Zeus's rule against gods and humans tampering with life and death. To punish Asclepius, Zeus struck him with a thunderbolt

The Greek healing god Asclepius cures a patient in this sculpture.

crafted by the Cyclopes. The healer died. Angry over the death of his son, Apollo wanted revenge against Zeus. Realizing he was no match for Zeus, Apollo instead killed the first generation of Cyclopes, who had made the weapon that slew his son.

The One Eyed Brutes of Hypereia

After the first generation of Cyclopes died, a second generation appeared on the island of Hypereia, now known as Sicily, in the Mediterranean Sea. The origins of the second generation are a mystery. Some said they sprung from drops of Uranus's blood that fell to the earth. Others said they were the offspring of Brontes, Steropes, and Arges. According to Homer, a Greek poet who lived in the eighth century B.C., at least one of these Cyclopes,

Polyphemus, was the offspring of Poseidon, the god of the sea, and a sea **nymph** named Thoosa.

The one-eyed giants of Hypereia were huge and powerful, but they were not as skilled or busy as the first generation of Cyclopes. They did not wear clothing but instead dressed themselves in animal skins. Rather than building homes of stone or wood, the one-eyed giants simply lived in empty caves. They did not bother with farming, either, but harvested whatever wild wheat, barley, and grapes happened to grow on their land.

Living off the land and taking whatever they wanted, the Cyclopes scorned **civil** society. "The Cyclopes have no assemblies for the making of laws, nor any settled customs," wrote Homer. "Each man is a lawgiver to his children and his wives, and nobody cares a jot for his neighbors."[3] The Cyclopes did not respect even the gods. "We Cyclopes do not care a jot for Zeus . . . nor for the rest of the blessed gods, since we are much stronger than they,"[4] one of the monsters boasted to a visitor to his island.

Killers Without a Conscience

The Cyclopes of Hypereia had no respect for human life. Homer told how one of the giants snatched up two men, killed them with his bare hands, and ate their flesh: "Limb by limb he tore them to pieces to make his meal, which he devoured like a mountain lion, never pausing till entrails and flesh, marrow and bones, were all consumed."[5]

A Cyclops devours a group of sailors that landed on his island.

With their enormous size and gruesome appetites, the one–eyed giants were a serious danger to humans. Luckily, the Cyclopes were bound to the island where they lived. "The Cyclopes have no ships, nor yet **shipwrights** who could make ships for them," wrote Homer, "they cannot therefore go from city to city, or sail over the sea to one another's country."[6] The only Greeks who had anything to fear of the Cyclopes were those who sailed to their island.

Unfortunately for one captain and crew, this is exactly what happened.

Chapter 2

Trapped on the Island of Cyclopes

Most people avoided the island where the Cyclopes lived. One Greek adventurer named Odysseus, however, could not resist finding out more about these strange creatures. It was a decision that Odysseus would live to regret.

Odysseus was the king of Ithaca, an island kingdom near the west coast of Greece. According to Homer, Odysseus was one of several Greek kings who went to war against Troy, a city located in what is now northwestern Turkey. After ten years of fighting, the Greeks finally sacked the city. The victors then sailed back to their homelands. Odysseus and his men headed for Ithaca, but a terrible storm blew their ships off course. "The force of the gusts tore

their sails to rags and tatters,"[7] Homer wrote in the *Odyssey*, his account of Odysseus's voyage home.

The winds blew for many days. The **wayfarers** sailed from island to island, eventually landing on one within sight of the island of the Cyclopes. Needing meat for their voyage, Odysseus and his men hunted and killed dozens of the wild goats that lived on the island. While they feasted, Odysseus and his men kept looking toward the land of the Cyclopes. Unable to resist his curiosity, Odysseus called a meeting and announced that he would visit the island.

Exploring the Island

Odysseus and his crew rowed across the narrow channel to the island of the Cyclopes. He took twelve of his best men ashore and told the rest of his crew to stay with the ship. Worried that he might find himself face-to-face with a Cyclops, Odysseus took along a strong wine that he thought he could use to drug the monster.

Odysseus and his followers crept up a cliff and found the entrance of a large cave that belonged to a Cyclops. The one-eyed creature kept herds of goats and sheep, milked them, and made cheese. Od-ysseus's men begged their leader to let them steal some cheese, lambs, and goats and return to the ship, but Odysseus refused. "It would have been far better so, I was not to be persuaded," Odysseus admitted, "I wished to see the owner of the cave and had hopes of some friendly gifts from my host."[8]

The Cyclops Polyphemus, who terrorized Odysseus and his men, stands at the entrance to his cave.

Odysseus was wrong. The Cyclops who lived in the cave had no interest in visitors, except to make a meal of them. Even worse, he blocked the exit to the cave with a huge boulder to keep his goats and sheep penned in. Odysseus and his men were trapped.

Death at the Hands of the Cyclops

After the Cyclops milked his goats, he lit a fire and saw Odysseus and his men. "Strangers!" the Cyclops bellowed when he saw the intruders. "Who may you be? Where do you hail from?" Odysseus answered: "We are Greeks on our way back from Troy." Odysseus added that he hoped their giant host would make them feel welcome. "We . . . hope that you may give us some friendly entertainment or even go further in your generosity,"[9] said Odysseus.

The monster was not impressed with the visitors. He snatched up two of them, bashed their skulls on the ground, and ate them while their companions watched in horror.

Later that evening the Cyclops fell asleep. Odysseus thought hard about his next move. He and his men still had their swords, so they might be able to kill the sleeping giant. But that would be useless, Odysseus realized, because the men lacked the strength to move the boulder. With the Cyclops dead, the men would be trapped inside the cave. The clever Odysseus decided that it would be wiser to blind the creature.

The next morning, the Cyclops killed and ate two more of the Greeks. Then the giant left to tend his animals, making sure to replace the great rock so the men could not escape. While the giant was gone, Odysseus took a large piece of olive wood that the Cyclops had set aside to use as a club and cut off a length of it. He then had his men shave down one end of the beam. Odysseus finished sharpening the point himself, then placed it in a fire to harden it. The spear completed, Odysseus waited for the Cyclops to return.

"Nobody" Tricks the Monster

When the Cyclops returned to the cave, he again milked his animals. The creature then killed and ate

Odysseus's men hide from Polyphemus beneath the giant's sheep in this seventeenth-century painting.

The clever Odysseus pours wine for the Cyclops, hoping to get him drunk.

two more of Odysseus's crew members. Odysseus decided it was time to spring his trap. He poured out a bowlful of his special, strong wine and called to the monster. "Here, Cyclops," Odysseus said, "have some wine to wash down that meal of human flesh."[10]

The greedy monster slurped down the wine with delight. "Be good enough," the monster said, "to let me have some more; and tell me your name, here and now, so that I may make you a gift that you will value."[11]

Odysseus gladly poured three more servings of wine for the Cyclops, but he decided not to tell the monster his real name. Instead, Odysseus said his

name was "Nobody." The giant then revealed what his present would be: "I will eat Nobody last, and the rest before him. That shall be your gift."[12]

As the Cyclops finished speaking, the powerful wine overtook him. Reeling under the influence of the alcohol, the giant dropped to the ground and passed out. This was the moment Odysseus had waited for. He placed the end of the spear into the fire and heated it until the green wood was almost ablaze. He withdrew the weapon from the fire, then he and his men attacked the Cyclops. "Seizing the olive pole, they drove its sharpened end into the Cyclop's eye, while I used my weight from

Odysseus and his men blind Polyphemus by driving a stake into the Cyclops's eye.

above to twist it home, like a man boring a ship's timber with a drill,"[13] Odysseus recalled.

The Wounded Giant

The Cyclops awoke screaming from the pain in his eye. As Odysseus and his men hid, the giant clawed at his eye and pulled out the spear. The attack worked. The great creature was blind in its only eye.

The monster's shouting awakened the other Cyclopes, who lived in neighboring caves. Some of them gathered outside the cave's entrance and asked, "What on earth is wrong with you, Polyphemus?"[14] (This is how Odysseus and his men discovered the giant's name.) At this, the wounded creature remembered the name Odysseus had given him and shouted that "Nobody" was hurting him. If nobody was hurting him, the other Cyclopes asked, why was he making such a fuss? Thinking Polyphemus to be a nuisance, the other Cyclopes returned to their own caves.

All Actions Have Consequences

The next morning, the blinded giant had to roll back the huge rock to let his animals out to graze. He wanted to make sure that the intruders who had maimed him did not escape, so he crouched down

Opposite: Odysseus and his men sneak out of Polyphemus's cave as the blind monster tries to find them.

near the entranceway. If any of the men tried to sneak past him, he would feel them with his huge hands and crush them.

The crafty Odysseus weighed various possible plans. Finally, he decided to use the monster's own sheep to make an escape. Each of the Greeks quietly clutched the underside of a sheep and held on tight to the wool. As the sheep walked out of the cave, Odysseus later recalled, the Cyclops "passed his hands along the backs of the animals . . . but the idiot never noticed that my men were . . . under the breasts of his own woolly sheep."[15]

Polyphemus throws giant rocks in an attempt to sink Odysseus's ship.

The Son of a God

The Greeks escaped the clutches of Polyphemus, but they still were not safe. They crept down to their ship and slowly pulled away from land. Once again Odysseus made a mistake. Believing he and his men were safe, Odysseus decided to tell the blind giant what he thought of him. Calling out from the ship, Odysseus taunted Polyphemus. Enraged, the Cyclops broke off the top of a mountain and hurled it in the direction of Odysseus's voice, barely missing the ship.

Odysseus's crew begged their leader to be quiet, but Odysseus called out again, "Cyclops, if anyone ever asks you how you came by your unsightly blindness, tell him your eye was put out by Odysseus, Sacker of Cities, who lives in Ithaca!"[16] This time Polyphemus did something worse than throw a piece of a mountain. The monster that had mocked the gods now asked for their help. Polyphemus called upon his father, Poseidon, to take revenge on the Greeks.

Unfortunately for Odysseus, Poseidon heard his blind son's plea. In the months and years to come, the god

Odysseus and his men sail away from the island of the Cyclopes in this English painting.

of the sea caused a great deal of trouble for the king of Ithaca. All of Odysseus's men were killed later in the voyage, and it took him ten long years to make it back home. His encounter with the Cyclops showed that all actions, whether good or ill, have consequences. Odysseus outwitted the monster, but he paid a high price for taunting his enemy.

Chapter 3

Disturbing the Dreams of Generations

In the centuries since Homer composed the *Odyssey,* the story of the Cyclops has enchanted, entertained, and frightened generations of readers. It also has inspired other artists to depict the fearsome giant in their own paintings, sculptures, plays, and motion pictures.

Archaeologists have found a painting of Odysseus and his men blinding the Cyclops on pottery that dates back to 650 B.C. The Greek playwright Euripides wrote a play about the monster in 408 B.C. The Romans, who later conquered the Greeks, depicted the Cyclopes in mosaics on floors and walls. Italian painters of the Renaissance were also fascinated by the Cyclopes. In 1525 Giulio Romano painted a

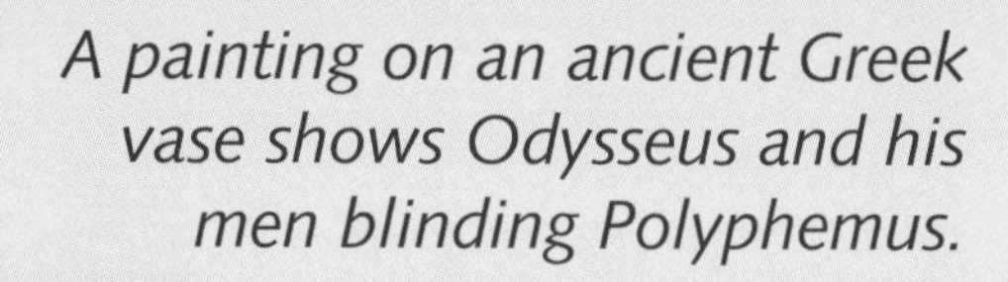

A painting on an ancient Greek vase shows Odysseus and his men blinding Polyphemus.

breathtaking portrait of Polyphemus sitting in his cave. Seventy years later, Annibale Carracci painted a **fresco** of the giant about to hurl the mountaintop at Odysseus. Modern artists such as Gustave Moreau and Odilon Redon also painted the one–eyed creature.

The Eye of the Camera Focuses on Cyclops

With the birth of motion pictures and television, filmmakers were always searching for stories of adventure that could be told through the eye of a camera. Not surprisingly, they have turned to one of the greatest adventure tales ever written, the *Odyssey.* Two large–scale versions of the *Odyssey* have made it to the screen. The first, *Ulysses,* made in 1954, starred Kirk Douglas as Ulysses, the Roman name of Odysseus. The other, a TV miniseries produced in 1997, featured Armand Assante as Odysseus. Both movies included the famous sequence in which Odysseus and his men encounter and outwit the Cyclops.

In both of these films, the Cyclops was played by a human actor wearing a costume and makeup. Effective makeup was the key to making the character seem real. After all, the main feature that set the Cyclops apart from other characters was his single eye. If his eye looked phony, audiences would not take the character or the film seriously.

To create the illusion of a single–eyed being, the film's makeup artist had to do two things. The first was to cover the actor's own eyes. The other was to

The enormous Cyclops enters his cave in a scene from the 1954 film Ulysses.

attach an artificial single eye. The makeup artist achieved both goals at once by using a piece of latex rubber called an appliance.

To make the appliance, the makeup artist first made a plaster copy–a sort of bust–of the actor's face. The artist then applied modeling clay to the bust to mold the Cyclops's special features. When the clay face matched the artist's vision of the Cyclops, the makeup artist covered it in wet plaster. When the plaster dried, he separated it from the clay face. Now he had a plaster mold of the clay face. Into this mold

Skillful use of makeup turned the actor playing Polyphemus in Ulysses *into a hideous Cyclops.*

the artist painted or poured liquid latex. After the latex became solid, he removed the finished appliance, painted it skin color, and added hair and other details. Attached to the actor's face with special glue, the appliance covered the actor's real eyes. (The actor could see through small slits cut in the appliance.) From the middle of the new, artificial forehead glared a single, gleaming eye. With a wig of long, matted hair and an animal–skin costume, the actor looked like the mythical Cyclops.

Visual Tricks Make a Giant

To make the Cyclops look like a giant, the director and camera operator used several tricks. One trick was to place the actor playing the Cyclops on one side of the frame (the image seen through the camera lens and on the screen) and place Odysseus and his men on the other side of the frame. Because the actors playing Odysseus and his men were standing much farther away from the camera than the actor playing the Cyclops, they looked much smaller than the monster. Lined up correctly, such shots create the illusion that all the characters are standing at the same distance from the camera but that one towers over the rest.

The 1997 version of the *Odyssey* used a technique known as Computer Generated Imagery or CGI. Using CGI, filmmakers combine two images into one. In the case of the Cyclops, they first filmed the actor playing the monster on a set designed to look

like the inside of a cave. The actor looked down at his feet and spoke toward the empty floor. A technician scanned this image into a computer. Then the technician scanned in an image of the actors playing the men. Finally, using a computer, the technician combined the two images, making the men the appropriate size and placing them near the Cyclops's feet.

The Cyclops Travels Outside the Odyssey

Cyclopes proved to be such frightening creatures that others have used them in their works, as well. For example, television writer Carey Wilber included an encounter with Cyclopes in an episode of the popular television series *Lost in Space.* Airing in October 1965, the episode "There Were Giants in the Earth" told how the crew of the *Jupiter 2* spaceship landed on a planet inhabited by a race of Cyclopes. On this planet two crew members, Professor John Robinson and Major Don West, encountered a Cyclops. The unarmed men hid in a cave to escape from the giant. Using special equipment, ten-year-old Will Robinson, John Robinson's son, noticed that his father and Major West were in trouble. He grabbed a laser gun, rushed to the cave, and used the gun to stun the Cyclops. The entire crew then escaped in a roving vehicle.

As in the *Odyssey,* the *Lost in Space* Cyclops broke off a huge piece of a mountain and hurled it toward the escaping crew of explorers. This scene was the

subject of a plastic model kit manufactured by the Aurora Toy Company in the 1960s. Recently the Polar Lights company created its own model version of the Cyclops's attack on the Robinson family.

Sinbad and the Cyclops

The most colorful and exciting movie depicting the Cyclops was based loosely on Homer's *Odyssey*. It told the story of the *Arabian Nights* hero, Sinbad the sailor. In 1958, the film *The Seventh Voyage of Sinbad* introduced the public to the most menacing Cyclops ever seen on stage or screen.

The Polar Lights company manufactures this model of the Lost in Space *cyclops.*

This Cyclops was not a man in a monster suit. Instead, it was a miniature model created by special-effects wizard Ray Harryhausen. To make his creature look scary, Harryhausen gave his Cyclops special features in addition to the single, staring eye. Harryhausen's Cyclops had a huge horn projecting from its head. Rather than human legs, it had the legs of a goat, just as the ancient Greek god Pan had. Harryhausen later explained: "I was . . . striving to give the appearance that the Cyclops wasn't a man in a suit. And I thought that the **cloven** hooves and the lower quarters of a goat would help to aid that."[17]

Bringing the Figure to Life

To make his model of the Cyclops appear to move, Harryhausen used a technique known as stop-motion animation. Built with a metal skeleton and moveable miniature joints, the Cyclops figurine could take any pose Harryhausen wanted. To make the creature appear to move, Harryhausen placed the model on a miniature set and set up his camera nearby. The camera allowed Harryhausen to shoot a single frame of film at a time. Normally a camera photographs at a rate of twenty-four frames per second. Each frame is like a still photo. But when the film runs in a projector at twenty-four frames a second, the images on the frames speed by and the eye is fooled into seeing motion.

Opposite: Ray Harryhausen created this terrifying horned Cyclops for the 1958 film The Seventh Voyage of Sinbad.

Taking advantage of this illusion, Harryhausen placed his Cyclops in the desired pose, stepped back, and snapped a single frame of film. Then he returned to the model. Carefully, he moved some of the creature a tiny bit and snapped another frame. Time after time, he repeated this process, slowly making the model Cyclops move through all the poses called for in the scene. The thousands of individual photos taken of the model were then projected at normal speed. The tiny sculpture appeared to walk, jump, wave its arms, snarl, and attack.

The Cyclops was just part of the action, of course. To make a realistic movie, the creature had to interact with the human actors. To achieve this effect, the film's director shot scenes of the actors on location. There, they looked at, fought with, or ran away from nothing, all the while pretending they saw a real Cyclops. Harryhausen projected these film clips of the actors onto a small screen built into his miniature set. Each time he made a tiny change in the model Cyclops's position and snapped a frame of film, he advanced the film of the live actors by one frame. In this way, the live–action and miniature–action shots came together and matched each other. When the film was shown in theaters, the human actors seemed to interact with a giant, living Cyclops.

The Seventh Voyage of Sinbad was a huge success. Coming in the midst of the monster movie craze of the 1950s and early 1960s, Harryhausen's Cyclops was featured alongside such monsters as the Mummy,

Frankenstein, and Godzilla in monster magazines, in packs of trading cards, and as toy figurines. *Famous Monsters Magazine* number 118 featured Harryhausen's one-horned Cyclops on its cover. In 1961, the Nu-Card company released a pack of sixty-six horror monster trading cards with pictures of famous monsters on the front and "Horrible Jokes" on the back. Card number 49 featured "Cyclops from 'Sinbad the Sailor.'" In 1964 the Palmer toy company released a set of eight monster figurines that included King Kong, Dracula, and Harryhausen's Cyclops. The plastic figurine showed the one-eyed giant squatting on its hind legs, staring at its unseen enemies with its naked, **bulbous** eye.

Harryhausen's Cyclops prepares to attack Sinbad on a beach in a scene from the film.

More recently Wizard Books introduced a set of playing cards. One card in the 2004 Monster series is the "magically animated Iron Cyclops."[18] Players use the Cyclops and other cards to compete in games.

Using the Eye for Laughs

The Cyclopes that have turned up in recent motion pictures have been more funny than scary. The 2001 animated movie *Monsters, Inc.* featured a one-eyed monster named Mike Wazowski. Created by Pixar Animation Studios and voiced by comedian Billy Crystal, Mike is the joke-cracking

A miniature Cyclops and a horned monster, the stars of Monsters, Inc.*, pose for a photo.*

sidekick of James P. "Sulley" Sullivan, the scariest creature in Monstropolis. A Cyclops also makes a brief appearance in the 2004 movie *Shrek 2.* In his first scene, the creature peers out a peephole in the door. When he opens the door, the audience sees that he was looking through the peephole with his only eye. Even in these lighthearted moments, the Cyclops is meant to startle and surprise.

To a baby crawling on the floor, adults appear as giants–large, loud, and unpredictable. Memories of those times may be one reason why many young children have a fear of giants and why stories about giants continue to be told around the world. Most of the giants in myths and legends look like oversized people with regular human faces. Their sheer size makes them scary. A giant with a **distorted** face–especially with one eye instead of two–is even more frightening than other giants. When that one-eyed giant **gorges** itself on human flesh, as the Cyclops does, it is certain to remain one of the most terrifying creatures ever to come from the human imagination.

Notes

Chapter One: The Terror of Greece

1. Quoted in Hillary Mayell, "Cyclops Myth Spurred by 'One–Eyed' Fossils?" *National Geographic News,* February 5, 2003. http://news.nationalgeographic.com/news/2003/02/0205_030205_cyclops.html.
2. Hesiod, *Theogony,* in *Hesiod and Theognis,* trans. Dorothea Wender. New York: Penguin, 1973, pp. 45–46.
3. Homer, *Odyssey,* trans. E.V. Rieu. Baltimore: Penguin, 1961, p. 142.
4. Homer, *Odyssey,* p. 146.
5. Homer, *Odyssey,* p. 147.
6. Homer, *Odyssey,* trans. Samuel Butler, New York: Barnes & Noble, 1993, p. 162.

Chapter Two: Trapped on the Island of Cyclopes

7. Homer, *Odyssey,* p. 141.
8. Homer, *Odyssey,* p. 145.
9. Homer, *Odyssey,* p. 146.
10. Homer, *Odyssey,* p. 148.
11. Homer, *Odyssey,* p. 149.
12. Homer, *Odyssey,* p. 149.

13. Homer, *Odyssey*, pp. 149–50.
14. Homer, *Odyssey*, p. 150.
15. Homer, *Odyssey*, p. 151.
16. Homer, *Odyssey*, p. 153.

Chapter Three: Disturbing the Dreams of Generations

17. Quoted in Jeff Roven, *From the Land Beyond Beyond: The Films of Willis O'Brien and Ray Harryhausen*. New York: Berkley, 1977, pp. 131, 134.
18. Wizard Books, www.fightingfantasygamebooks.com/files/tradingcards/2.jpg.

Glossary

archaeologist: A person who studies prehistoric people and their cultures.
Bronze Age: A period of human culture between the Stone Age and the Iron Age, characterized by the use of weapons and implements made of bronze.
bulbous: Resembling a bulb in shape; rounded or swollen.
civil: In accordance with organized society.
cloven: Split into two parts.
distorted: Changed, twisted, or exaggerated.
feud: A bitter quarrel or dispute.
fresco: A painting made on wet plaster.
gorges: Eats a great deal in a single meal.
nymph: A magical being found in trees, water, mountains, and other things in nature.
shipwrights: Builders of ships.
***Theogony*:** Hesiod's account of the origin and family history of the gods.
wayfarers: Travelers.

For Further Exploration

Books

Ancient Sources

Hesiod, *Theogony,* in *Hesiod and Theognis*. Trans. Dorothea Wender. New York: Penguin, 1973. The story of the creation of the world and the gods and their offspring (including the Cyclopes), as told by an ancient Greek.

Homer, *Odyssey*. Trans. E.V. Rieu. Baltimore: Penguin, 1961. One of the best and easiest–to–read versions of Homer's classic tale of the wanderings of the Greek hero Odysseus.

Modern Sources

David Bellingham, *An Introduction to Greek Mythology*. Secaucus, NJ: Chartwell Books, 1989. A basic introduction to the characters and events of Greek mythology.

Warwick Hutton, *Odysseus and the Cyclops*. New York: Margaret K. McElderry, 1995. Well illustrated, this is an effective retelling of the episode from the *Odyssey* in which Odysseus outwits the Cyclops.

Don Nardo, *Greek Mythology*. San Diego: KidHaven,

2002. Retells some of the classic ancient Greek myths for young readers.

Jeff Roven, *From the Land Beyond Beyond: The Films of Willis O'Brien and Ray Harrihausen.* New York: Berkley, 1977. A fascinating look at the films of the two greatest stop–motion animators of the twentieth century. The volume includes an entire chapter on *The Seventh Voyage of Sinbad,* with its great movie Cyclops.

Internet Sources

Calliope, "The Blinding of Polyphemus," (www.calliope.free–online.co.uk/odyssey/od11.htm.) An easy–to–read version of the scene from Homer's *Odyssey* in which the Greeks blind the giant Cyclops, enlivened with several images of the scene by ancient Greek artists.

FortuneCity.com, "The Seventh Voyage of Sinbad," (http://lavender.fortunecity.com/judidench/584/new–7thv.html). Part of a tribute to movie specials– effects wizard Ray Harryhausen, this site contains a lot of information about the film in which Harryhausen's Cyclops appears, including information about the cast and crew, a look behind the scenes, and images and sounds from the film.

Greek Mythology.com, "Cyclopes," (www.greekmythology.com/Myths/Creatures/Cyclopes/cyclopes.html). A basic summary of the mythical Cyclopes, with several links leading to related materials and background stories.

Index

Picture Credits

Cover: © Scala/Art Resource
© Alexander Burkatovski/CORBIS, 19
© CORBIS, 21
© COREL Corporation, 8
© Erich Lessing/Art Resource, NY, 5, 11, 26
© Lux Film/Kobal Collection, 29
© Mike Maass, 33
© Mary Evans Picture Library, 14, 17, 20
© Gianni Dagli Orti/CORBIS, 12
© Photofest, 30, 34, 37
© Scala/Art Resource, 23, 28
© Skulls Unlimited International, 7
© Tate Gallery, London/Art Resource, 6
© Frank Trapper/CORBIS, 38
© Sandro Vannini/CORBIS, 8 (inset)
www.artrenewal.org, 24–25

About the Author

Historian and award-winning author Don Nardo has written or edited many books about the ancient Greeks, including *Greek and Roman Sport, Life in Ancient Athens,* the *Greenhaven Encyclopedia of Greek and Roman Mythology,* and the four-volume *Library of Ancient Greece.* He lives with his wife Christine in Massachusetts.

A widely published poet and playwright, Bradley Steffens is the author and coauthor of twenty-five books for young adults, including *Loch Ness Monster* and *Fall of the Roman Empire.* He lives in Escondido, California, with his wife Angela.